The Magic School Bus
PRESENTS
Our Solar System

Scholastic Inc.

Previous page: The surface of the Sun

ISBN 978-0-545-68365-4

Produced by Potomac Global Media, LLC

All text, illustrations, and compilations © 2014 Scholastic Inc.
Based on The Magic School Bus series © Joanna Cole and Bruce Degen
Text by Tom Jackson Illustrations by Carolyn Bracken
Consultant: Carole Stott, astronomer and space-science writer, England

Published by Scholastic Inc., 557 Broadway, New York, NY 10012.

12 11 10 9 8 7 6 5 4 3 2 1   14 15 16 17 18 19/0

Cover design by Paul Banks
Interior design by Thomas Keenes
Photo research by Sharon Southren

Printed in the U.S.A.   40
First printing, July 2014

Contents

p. 12

p. 22

p. 24

Our Solar System

We got to school really early. The Sun had not come up yet and we could see stars in the dark sky above us. "Today we are going to learn about the solar system," said Ms. Frizzle. The solar system is our little patch of space. The Sun sits in the middle of it, while Earth and the other planets orbit the Sun.

The Sun rises every morning and sets at night. But the Sun is not moving. It is Earth that moves — it rotates once every 24 hours.

Planets look like bright stars. Each one follows its own path across the sky.

BLAST OFF!

4

It's a name game!
Name that planet!

Planets and their names
by Carlos

Besides Earth, there are seven planets in the solar system. Humans have known about the five nearest planets for thousands of years — they can be seen with just our eyes. The two farthest planets were only discovered after astronomers started using telescopes to study the sky. Ancient people named the planets after their gods. Today, we use the names of Greek and Roman gods and goddesses for all of the planets except Earth. Our planet's name comes from an old English word, "erthe," meaning "ground."

Sweeping lights
The stars are set in fixed patterns called constellations. As Earth rotates, the constellations seem to sweep slowly across the sky at night.

Shining bright
The stars are so far away that it takes years for their light to reach Earth.

Frizzle Fact
Our Sun is not the only star with planets in orbit around it. Scientists think that at least 1 in every 20 stars in the universe has a few planets of its own.

The Sun

The Sun sends out a "solar wind" of hot gas into space. One million tons (almost one million tonnes) of gas blow away every second.

Flame cloud
Huge loops of hot gas burst out from the Sun's surface. This one is as high as about twenty Earths all lined up in a row.

Glowing crown
The Sun is surrounded by a glowing outer layer called the corona, which means "crown." It is at least 8 million miles (13 million kilometers) deep.

No solid ground
The Sun is a huge ball of superhot gases called plasma. The plasma bubbles at the surface, a bit like boiling water.

The Sun is a star. It is the nearest star to Earth and by far the brightest object in the sky. It provides all the light and heat in the solar system. The Sun's surface is 9,900 degrees Fahrenheit (5,500 degrees Celsius), which is hot enough to melt our entire planet.

Scorching hot!

Two or three times a year, the Moon passes directly between Earth and the Sun, blocking some or all of the Sun's light and causing a solar eclipse. When all of the Sun's light is blocked, it is called a total solar eclipse.

Why is the Sun so hot?
by Keesha

The Sun, like other stars, produces heat and light by a process called nuclear fusion, which happens at the Sun's center. The Sun consists mainly of hydrogen, a simple substance made of tiny units called atoms. During fusion, the atoms are squeezed so tightly that they join or fuse together. When this happens, they make larger atoms of a substance called helium. The process creates enormous amounts of energy that shine out as the Sun's light and heat.

The Sun gets spots! These are darker patches on the surface, where the temperature has dropped. Most sunspots are larger than Earth.

Frizzle Fact

It takes 100,000 years for the heat produced at the Sun's center (the core) to reach its surface. It takes eight minutes for the Sun's heat to reach Earth.

Mercury

Mercury is the smallest planet in the solar system. It is just one-third the size of Earth. Mercury is also the nearest planet to the Sun, and takes just 88 days to go all the way around it. It is difficult to see Mercury from Earth because the Sun's glare often hides it.

Mercury has the biggest temperature drop in the solar system. By day, the Sun's heat could melt lead. After sunset, it is cold enough to turn Earth's air to liquid.

Mercury rotates very slowly. Each rotation takes 59 days.

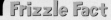

Frizzle Fact

Mercury is named after the speedy Roman messenger god. The planet moves very quickly in its orbit. It is rarely seen in the night sky.

Mercury has hardly any atmosphere because there are no gases surrounding it.

Bright star
From Mercury, the Sun looks more than twice the size that it does from Earth and is six times brighter.

Clouds? In space?

How did the planets form?
by Wanda

Mercury is a rocky planet, as are Venus, Earth, and Mars. The other planets are made from gas and liquid and are often called gas giants. All the planets formed from a cloud of dust and gases left over when the Sun formed around 5 billion years ago. The heavier dust was closer to the Sun and the lighter gases farther out. The specks slowly clumped together and, after hundreds of millions of years, formed the eight planets: the rocky ones near the Sun and the gas ones farther out.

Cratered surface
Of all the planets, Mercury has the most craters, or large dips. They formed when space rocks smashed into the planet billions of years ago.

Venus

Hottest place
Venus is the hottest planet in the solar system. At 867 degrees Fahrenheit (464 degrees Celsius) its surface is much hotter than a standard kitchen oven.

Venus is the second closest planet to the Sun and the planet nearest to Earth. It is covered in thick white clouds, which reflect sunlight. This makes Venus sparkle more brightly than any star. The clouds also hide the planet's surface. Space probes use radar to see through them.

From Earth, we can see Venus (pictured above the Moon in this image) just as the Sun sets or rises. Venus is often called the Morning or Evening Star.

It's always dark here. Hardly any light shines through the clouds.

Maat Mons, Venus's largest volcano, as photographed by the Magellan space probe.

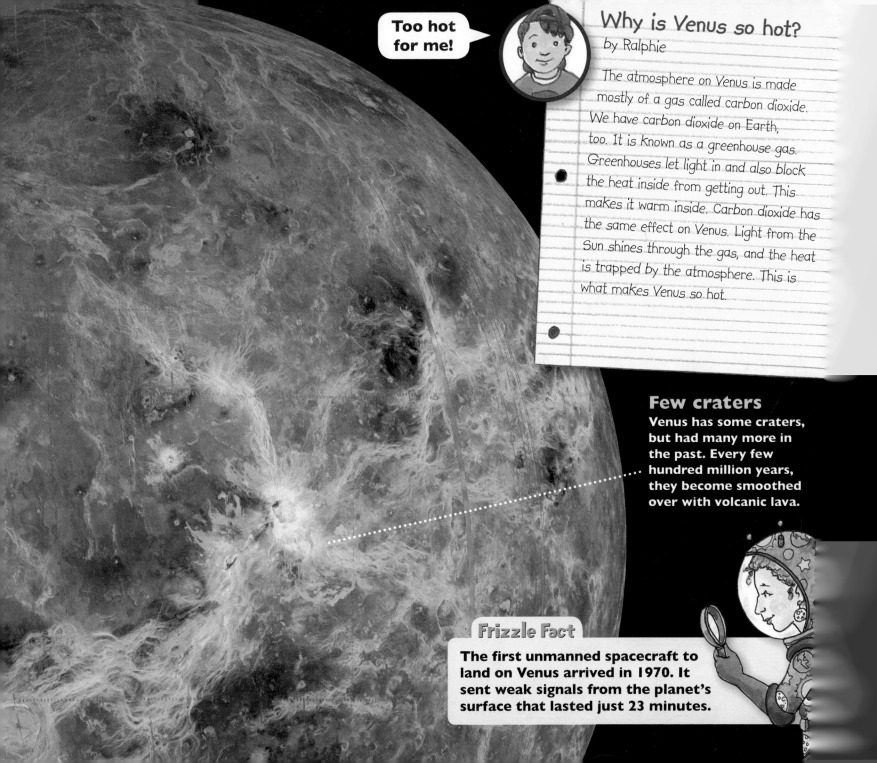

Too hot for me!

Why is Venus so hot?
by Ralphie

The atmosphere on Venus is made mostly of a gas called carbon dioxide. We have carbon dioxide on Earth, too. It is known as a greenhouse gas. Greenhouses let light in and also block the heat inside from getting out. This makes it warm inside. Carbon dioxide has the same effect on Venus. Light from the Sun shines through the gas, and the heat is trapped by the atmosphere. This is what makes Venus so hot.

Few craters
Venus has some craters, but had many more in the past. Every few hundred million years, they become smoothed over with volcanic lava.

Frizzle Fact
The first unmanned spacecraft to land on Venus arrived in 1970. It sent weak signals from the planet's surface that lasted just 23 minutes.

Earth

Solar wind is captured near the North and South Poles. The high-speed blast hitting the air creates an amazing light show called an aurora or, in the Northern Hemisphere, the northern lights.

Landmasses

Dry land occurs wherever the planet's rocky outer crust is thick enough to poke out of the oceans.

Water planet

The oceans cover more than two-thirds of Earth's surface. Scientists think the water arrived billions of years ago and that it came out of the ground as steam. It then formed the oceans.

Earth looks pale blue when viewed from space.

Stormy weather

Earth's atmosphere is made up of areas of hot and cold air. When they meet each other, rain clouds and storms form.

Earth is special. It is the only place in the universe known to have liquid water on its surface. Earth is also the only place with signs of life. The planet's position in the solar system is sometimes called the "Goldilocks orbit" — it has seasons that are neither too hot nor too cold, but just right for life to survive.

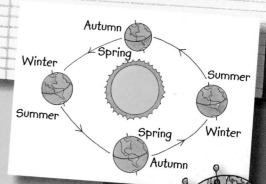

The seasons
by Dorothy Ann

Most places on Earth experience four seasons: winter, spring, summer, and fall. The seasons occur because Earth is not upright, but tipped over compared to its path around the Sun. For six months of the year, the northern half of Earth is tipped toward the Sun, making it warm. For the rest of the year the southern half of Earth points toward the Sun, making it warmer there and colder in the north.

Autumn
Spring
Winter
Summer
Summer
Spring
Winter
Autumn

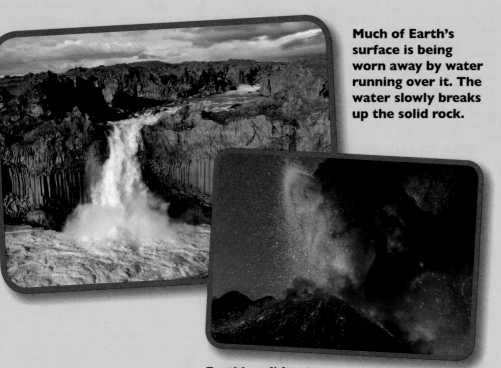

Much of Earth's surface is being worn away by water running over it. The water slowly breaks up the solid rock.

Earth's solid outer surface floats on a layer of magma, or hot melted rock. A volcano forms where the magma breaks through.

Frizzle Fact

Earth is like a giant magnet. There is liquid iron in its core, which moves in a spinning motion. Scientists believe this motion creates Earth's magnetism.

The Moon

Only 12 people have ever walked on the Moon. This astronaut is Charles M. Duke Jr., lunar module pilot of the Apollo 16 mission, which landed on the Moon in April 1972.

Earth has a companion. The Moon is our planet's only natural satellite — that's an object that travels around it. It may have formed when a small planet smashed into Earth about four billion years ago. You can see the Moon day or night, but it shows up best after sunset.

Mountain view
The Moon's mountains can be seen from Earth. They appear paler than the dark seas that cover the low-lying areas.

Footprints stay put on the Moon. There is no atmosphere, so there is no wind or rain to wipe them away.

Let's moonwalk!

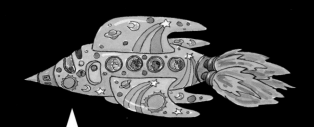

You can't get seasick on the Moon!

Does the Moon really have seas?
by Tim

Looking up at the Moon, we can see several dark patches on its surface. Since ancient times, astronomers have called these "lunar seas." They have names like the Sea of Tranquility and Ocean of Storms. But the Moon has no water! These seas are actually vast areas of dark rock that erupted from volcanoes when the Moon was much younger — and hotter. There are no volcanoes on the Moon now, but it does have moonquakes from time to time.

The Moon rotates at the same speed that it takes to orbit Earth, so the same side always faces Earth and we never see the back side.

Lunar module
This Apollo lunar module has room for two people. At liftoff, only the cabin section flies back into space. The legs stay on the Moon. The last lunar mission was made in 1972.

Dust layer
The Moon's surface is covered in a deep layer of dust. It was made when space rocks smashed into the surface and broke up into tiny pieces.

It's silent on the Moon because there is no air to carry sound.

Mars

Mars's red color comes from its iron-rich rocks. The idea is that the iron rusted when there was water on the planet.

Dry valley

Kasei Valles is one of the longest valleys on Mars. Scientists think it was formed by water rushing through this area billions of years ago. There is no water here now.

Volcanic giants

Pavonis Mons is one of several giant volcanoes. The largest of Mars's volcanoes is three times taller than Mount Everest.

Deep canyon

Mars has a giant system of canyons called Valles Marineris. It's four times deeper than the Grand Canyon and would stretch right across the United States.

O
f all the planets in the solar system, Mars, the red planet, is most like Earth. If humans ever decide to visit another planet, they will almost certainly go to Mars first. For now, scientists use rovers — robotic spacecraft with wheels — to drive across Mars and find out more about its landscape.

Robot eye
Cameras and laser beams study Martian rocks. They are looking for signs of water, and even life, from past times.

Mars Rover

It's the size of a small car.

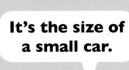

Rocky road
The six wheels move up and down. They can drive over rocky ground and through patches of sand.

Someday we could be Martians!

Could humans live on Mars?
by Phoebe

Mars is a harsh place. During the day it never gets hotter than 68 degrees Fahrenheit (20 degrees Celsius) and at night it can plunge to 193 degrees below zero (minus 125 degrees Celsius). That's much colder than Earth's South Pole. However, there is carbon dioxide on Mars, which is what plants need to grow. Astronauts could set up greenhouses there to grow food. Plants give out oxygen. One day, humans might be able to use plants to turn Mars into a small version of Earth.

Nuclear engine
A nuclear reactor powers the rover. The spacecraft is controlled by radio from Earth.

Frizzle Fact
Mars is a cold and completely dry red desert today, but scientists think seas and rivers once flowed over its surface.

Asteroid Belt

Between Mars and Jupiter there is a part of the solar system filled with rocks. This is the asteroid belt. Asteroids are rocks that orbit the Sun. They are much smaller than planets. There are billions of asteroids in the belt. Most are less than 12 miles (20 kilometers) across, but the largest asteroid, Ceres, is about the size of Texas.

Asteroids sometimes hit Earth. Most burn up as they rush through the air and become shooting stars. Space rocks that do hit the ground are called meteorites.

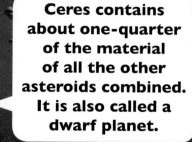

Ceres contains about one-quarter of the material of all the other asteroids combined. It is also called a dwarf planet.

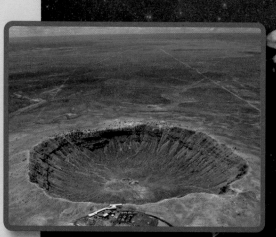

This crater in Arizona is just under 1 mile (1.6 kilometers) wide. The asteroid that made it was 150 feet (45 meters) across. It hit Earth 50,000 years ago.

Missing planet
The asteroids are the remains of a planet that failed to form between Mars and Jupiter when the solar system was very young.

Space rocks really rock!

What are asteroids made of?
by Arnold

Most asteroids are made from rock, others are a mixture of rock and metal, and the rest are just metal. These are the same kinds of materials that formed Earth and the other rocky planets about 4.5 billion years ago. Asteroids mainly made from metal probably came from the center of a small planet-like body that got smashed apart when the solar system was forming. The stony asteroids are probably made from the outer parts of the same, or a similar, body.

All shapes and sizes
Most asteroids are not round globes, but irregularly shaped rocks.

Distant light
The asteroid belt forms a donut-shaped ring around the Sun. It is around 100 million miles (161 million kilometers) thick, from its inner edge to its outer edge.

The first asteroid was spotted by telescope in 1801.

Frizzle Fact
The asteroid Ida is only about 30 miles (48 kilometers) wide but it still has its own tiny moon, called Dactyl.

Jupiter

Scientists say Jupiter's storms can last from about two hours to hundreds of years.

The Galileo spacecraft has spent many years studying Jupiter and its moons.

Cloud cover

Jupiter rotates every ten hours, which is very fast for something so large. The clouds separate into bands as it spins.

Stormy spot

There are many swirling storms in Jupiter's atmosphere. The largest is called the Great Red Spot.

White storm

This smaller, white storm is one of many that develop

Jupiter is a gas giant with 67 moons. It is the largest planet in the solar system (all the other planets could fit inside it). Jupiter's surface is not solid. The outer layer is made of gas, which gradually turns to liquid. Beneath this, there is a core of rocky and metallic material in the planet's center.

Can you spot the Red Spot?

The Great Red Spot
by Carlos

The Great Red Spot was first seen in the 1660s, not long after astronomers started using telescopes. It has been raging on Jupiter ever since. This big storm shows no sign of ending because it is constantly being fed with smaller storms that scoot around the atmosphere and end up joining the red spot. The winds inside the storm blow at 250 miles (400 kilometers) per hour. The huge red cloud bulges up about 5 miles (8 kilometers) above the surface of the planet.

The great pull of Jupiter's gravity creates volcanic activity on the moon Io. The moon has more volcanic eruptions than anywhere else in the solar system.

The moon Europa is completely covered by a sheet of water ice. There may be an ocean of liquid water beneath the surface.

Frizzle Fact

Lightning strikes in Jupiter's clouds are 12,500 miles (20,000 kilometers) long. They would flash halfway around Earth in a fraction of a second.

Saturn

Some of Saturn's rings are held in place by small moons, known as shepherd moons.

Visit from Earth
In 2004, a probe called *Cassini-Huygens* arrived at Saturn. It discovered some new moons and watched a storm on Saturn that raged for two years.

Separate rings
There are gaps in Saturn's rings. The largest is called the Cassini Division after Giovanni Cassini, the Italian astronomer who first saw the gap.

Bulging center
Saturn spins so quickly that it actually bulges in the middle.

22

Saturn is the second largest planet in the solar system. It is a gas giant, like Jupiter, and has pale bands of clouds covering its surface. Saturn is surrounded by enormous rings, which more than double the planet's width. These rings are 174,000 miles (280,000 kilometers) in diameter by less than 55 yards (50 meters) thick.

Rings of ice!

What are Saturn's rings made of?
by Keesha

Saturn's rings are made from billions of chunks of ice mixed with rock dust. The largest are about 30 feet (9 meters) across, but most are just an inch or two (a few centimeters) wide. Scientists think that the rings formed more recently than the planet, and that they were once joined together into an ice moon. The idea is that the gravity from Saturn pulled the ice moon in different directions, causing it to shatter.

The moon Mimas has a huge crater that takes up one-third of its width.

Saturn's largest moon is called Titan. It has lakes as big as America's Great Lakes. They do not contain water, but liquids similar to gasoline!

Frizzle Fact

Saturn's moon Enceladus has fountains made of water vapor and ice crystals that shoot out of cracks in the surface. They freeze to make a snowy shower.

Uranus and Neptune

The planets Uranus and Neptune are the most distant from the Sun. Their part of the solar system is much cooler, and some chemicals on these planets freeze solid. Both of these ice-cold giants have moons — Uranus has 27 and Neptune 14. Neptune's moon Triton is the largest of them all.

Uranus spins as if lying on its side, so it rolls around the Sun. The planet also has a system of faint rings.

Ice and dust

Triton's volcanoes erupt ice and slush rather than hot lava. The moon shoots plumes of dusty gas many miles into the sky.

Welcome to Neptune's moon Triton! The temperature is 391 degrees below zero Fahrenheit (minus 235 degrees Celsius).

It's one of the coldest places in the solar system.

Tiny Sun

From these ice-cold giants and their moons, the Sun is 900 times dimmer than it looks from Earth. Sunlight takes hours to reach these planets.

Ocean blue

Neptune is named after the Roman god of the sea. The name goes well with the deep blue color of the planet.

Hot gas!

What's inside an ice-cold giant?
by Ralphie

Beneath the planet's blue atmosphere is a deep, ocean-like layer. It is made from gases that are hot and tightly packed, and which act like a liquid. The planet's core is made of rock and metal.

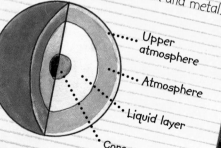

······ Upper atmosphere

······ Atmosphere

····· Liquid layer

···· Core

25

Icy Dwarfs and Comets

The solar system does not end at Neptune. Farther out is a tiny ice world called Pluto. It is one of several dwarf planets. The dwarfs belong to a belt of smaller icy objects. Beyond these are the comets.

Comets are chunks of snow and dust that come from the edges of the solar system. Every so often, a comet whizzes past the planets with two streaming tails.

Mystery world
Pluto's surface is thought to be like a dirty ice ball. This dwarf planet is a huge ball of ice with dust and rock mixed in.

Frizzle Fact
The idea for naming Pluto came from an 11-year-old English girl called Venetia. Pluto is the Roman god of the underworld.

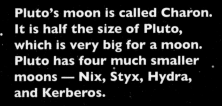

Pluto's moon is called Charon. It is half the size of Pluto, which is very big for a moon. Pluto has four much smaller moons — Nix, Styx, Hydra, and Kerberos.

Cosmic snowballs!

How come comets have tails?
by Wanda

Comets are made mostly from snow. Far away from the Sun, they are frozen solid, but when a comet gets closer to the Sun, heat from the Sun affects the comet's surface. The heat turns the snow to gas, and dust is released. The Sun's high-powered solar wind pushes the gas and dust away, to form two tails — one gas, one dust — that can be hundreds of millions of miles long!

Pluto and Charon are found in the Kuiper Belt. This region beyond the planets is filled with icy objects left over from when the planets were created.

Too cold for me!

Deep winter lasts for 60 years on Pluto. It gets so cold that the atmosphere freezes and falls as snow.

27

The Planets

Mercury
Width: 3,032 miles (4,879 kilometers)
One orbit of the Sun: 88 Earth days
One spin: 59 Earth days
Moons: 0
Named after: Roman messenger god
Distinctive features: Many craters, such as the Carolis Basin.

Venus
Width: 7,520 miles (12,103 kilometers)
One orbit of the Sun: 225 Earth days
One spin: 243 Earth days
Moons: 0
Named after: Roman goddess of love
Distinctive features: Thick clouds and acid rain.

Earth
Width: 7,926 miles (12,756 kilometers)
One orbit of the Sun: 365 days
One spin: 23.9 hours
Moons: 1
Named after: "erthe" (old English for "ground")
Distinctive feature: Oceans cover most of the surface.

Mars
Width: 4,228 miles (6,804 kilometers)
One orbit of the Sun: 687 Earth days
One spin: 24.6 hours
Moons: 2
Named after: Roman god of war
Distinctive feature: Mons Olympus is its largest volcano.

Jupiter

Width: 88,846 miles (142,984 kilometers)

One orbit of the Sun: 11.9 Earth years

One spin: 10 hours

Moons: 67

Named after: Roman king of the gods

Distinctive features: Great Red Spot storm; Ganymede (largest moon in the solar system).

Saturn

Width: 74,898 miles (120,536 kilometers)

One orbit of the Sun: 29.5 Earth years

One spin: 10.5 hours

Moons: 62

Named after: Roman god of time

Distinctive features: System of rings; Titan, the second largest moon in the solar system..

Uranus

Width: 31,763 miles (51,118 kilometers)

One orbit of the Sun: 84 Earth years

One spin: 17.25 hours

Moons: 27

Named after: Greek sky god

Distinctive feature: Orbits the Sun tilted on its side.

Neptune

Width: 30,775 miles (49,528 kilometers)

One orbit of the Sun: 165 Earth years

One spin: 16 hours

Moons: 14

Named after: Roman god of the sea

Distinctive features: High winds, faint rings, deep-blue color.

Well done, class! I hope you can join me on our next adventure!

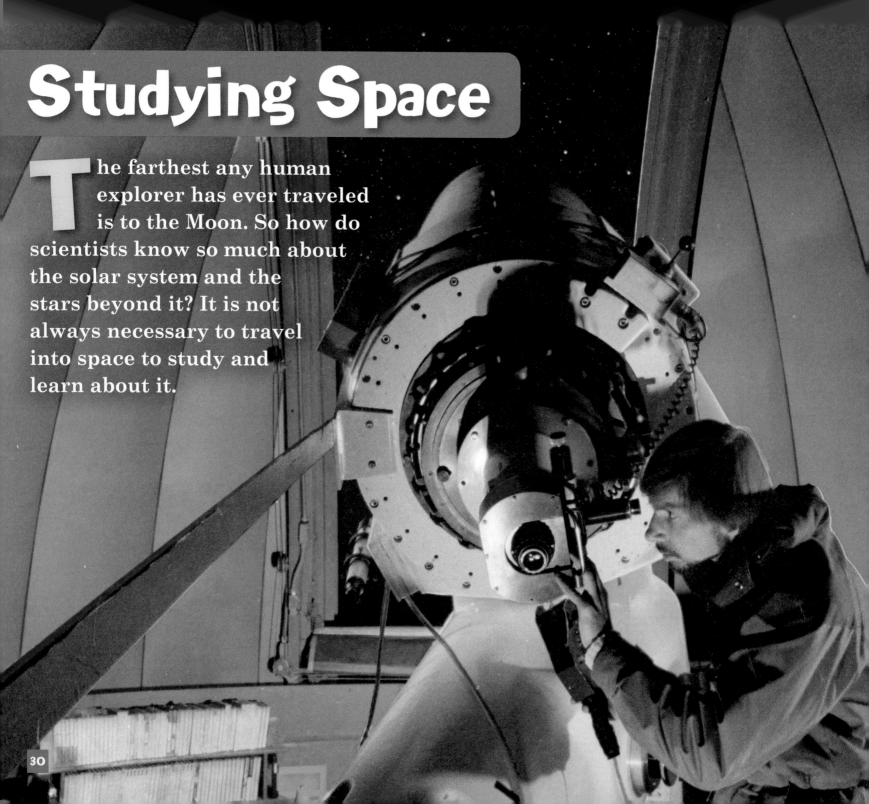

Studying Space

The farthest any human explorer has ever traveled is to the Moon. So how do scientists know so much about the solar system and the stars beyond it? It is not always necessary to travel into space to study and learn about it.

Astronomers

The science of space is called astronomy. There are many different types of astronomers. Some study the planets, while others look at the stars. They try to figure out how the universe was created and how it works. All astronomers do their work without leaving Earth. Instead they use several methods to collect information. Powerful telescopes allow them to peer deep into space and get a good look at its objects. Many of the objects in the solar system are too small to see clearly from Earth, so astronomers send probes into space. Probes can fly past comets and asteroids, they can go into orbit around planets or moons, and they can even land on the surface of an object.

Astronauts

People who go into space are known as astronauts, cosmonauts, or taikonauts depending on where they come from (the United States and Europe, Russia, or China, for example). The main job of an astronaut today is to learn more about the different effects that life in space can have on the human body. Over time astronauts hope to gather enough information so that, one day, it might be possible to send human crews deep into space to explore the solar system close-up.

Astrobiologists

One of the questions that astronomers ask time and again is whether life exists somewhere in the solar system, other than on Earth. Scientists called astrobiologists try to answer this question. They think about what kinds of life-forms might survive on alien worlds. Then they send probes to investigate some of those worlds and to see if the probes can find signs of life from the past. So far no aliens have ever been found.

Words to Know

Atmosphere The mixture of gases that surrounds a planet.

Atom The tiniest part of a material that has all the properties of that element. All matter in the universe is made up of atoms.

Comet A small snow and dust space body that travels around the Sun. Some get near the Sun and develop two long tails.

Core The most inner part of a planet. On Earth, the core is the intensely hot, most inner part of the planet.

Eclipse The effect achieved when one space body blocks the light of another. In an eclipse of the Moon, the Earth is directly between the Sun and the Moon. In an eclipse of the Sun, the Moon is directly between the Sun and the Earth, and blocks the Sun's light.

Gas A substance, such as air, that will spread to fill any space that contains it.

Gravity The force that pulls one object toward the center of another object and keeps it from floating away.

Magma Melted rock found beneath the Earth's surface. It is called lava when it flows out of volcanoes.

Orbit The curved path followed by a moon, planet, or satellite as it circles another larger space object.

Radar A way to find solid objects by reflecting radio waves off them and receiving the reflected waves. Radar is short for radio detection and ranging.

Rotate To move in a circle around a central point, like a wheel.

Satellite A moon or other space body that travels in an orbit around a larger space body.

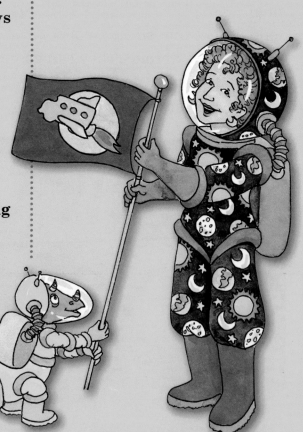